www.finishinglinepress.com

We Are Not a Museum
THE JEWS OF KOCHI

poems by

Pramila Venkateswaran

Finishing Line Press
Georgetown, Kentucky

We Are Not a Museum
THE JEWS OF KOCHI

"Some said that if you explored for long enough, you'd find your own story in one of the blue-and-white squares, because the pictures on the tiles could change, were changing, generation by generation, to tell the story of the Cochin Jews. Still others were convinced that the tiles were prophecies, the keys to whose meanings had been lost with the passing years."
—Salman Rushdie, *The Moor's Last Sigh*

ACKNOWLEDGMENTS

Some of the poems, with slight variations, have appeared in the following journals
and anthologies:

"Definition," *Inch magazine*
"Cemetery," *Poetica*
"From Israel to Kochi" nominated by *Poetica* for the Rosenberg prize
"Journey," *MAPS* (*Matwaala Anthology of Poetry by South Asian*s), 2019
"Exile" "The Face of the Other," and "History," *Erothanatos*
"Double Podia," *Life and Legends*
"Field Trip" and "Our Days are Like Passing Shadows," *Thirteen Days to Let Go*
(Aldrich 2011)
"I was Seven," *Leaves of Me,* Ed. Gladys Henderson and Peter Dugan, 2018
"The Clock Tower," *Performance Poets Literary Review*

I wish to thank my sister, Jayashree George, for the cover image. During our trip to
the Kochi synagogue, she was inspired to create compositions in water color and
ink. I wish to thank Nassau Community College for sabbatical leave, which enabled
me to travel to Kochi and Eranakulam exploring the synagogues as well as visit the
house where my family lived in Mattancherry, where the Kochi synagogue is located. I
thank Sally Drucker, Kathrine Jason, Richard Newman, and Ralph Nazareth, for their
comments on some of the poems. Many thanks to my family for believing in my work.

Publisher: Leah Huete de Maines
Editor: Christen Kincaid
Cover Art: Jayashree George
Author Photo: Pramila Venkateswaran
Cover Design: Elizabeth Maines McCleavy

Order online: www.finishinglinepress.com
also available on amazon.com

Author inquiries and mail orders:
Finishing Line Press
PO Box 1626
Georgetown, Kentucky 40324
USA

Table of Contents

Exile

Coming is always arduous
—mountains, near-death escapades

until you chalk a square space
and call it home.

Going happens in a split second,
a bird taking wing.

*

Once exiled from Palestine
it is hard to bear

yet another exile
even if winds are fair.

*

We have left a door open
in Kerala: its lit interior welcomes

our mornings. We turn east,
as once we turned toward Jerusalem.

The Long Journey

1

She bundled everything they owned: two skirts,
two blouses, a loaf of bread, dried

olives, figs, some meat,
a square cloth, two bowls,

Joseph's robe, the family Bible,
and a small sack of earth

to remind them where they came
from.

2

The earth carried the smell of
        trees, the light of the moon
        under which she prayed,

the sound of water.

She heard it call,
        come back.

Centuries later,
her progeny heeded its call.

3

        Hear her say,
           Just the rocking of the body
               a boat on the waters
           whisper of prayers
               a slight wind

               will us to live
           that day and sleep
               without a care;

just to find a place
          to call on Yahweh
          to enfold us

     keeps us full.

The Face of the Other

the face speaks to me and thereby
invites me to a relation...
Emmanuel Levinas, "Totality and Infinity"

Why do some see yellow stars
instead of faces, their marauding pens
marking the city's walls with swastikas?

Hate clouds barrel down the ages
from the Black Sea and Ararat, from the Nile
and Babylon. It storms in
among starched shirts and rags.

Why is a Jewish child selected
to be erased? Philosophers say
to love is to see the other in oneself. But
the other blends into the unknowable.

I ask, doesn't a child crying for his mom
on any street around the globe
make you wince?

Chorus: At the Palace of the Raja of Cochin

Rajadi Raja, your royal highness Ramavarma Kulashekara Perumal,
we bow before your blessed feet. The morning breezes bring
tidings of something new to our Keral coast. Men
and women with children arrive in boats, speaking a
tongue we have not heard before. They look like merchants
from Arabia, but are different. The men wear caps
on their heads and the women wear long, pale skirts,
have dark eyes like the apsaras in your court,
wear no ornaments in their dark brown and black hair,
and walk with a firm gait beside their men.

Rajadi Raja, the men are at the palace gates and ask
to pay their respects to you. They bear baskets of dried
fruit, dates, almonds, pistachios, apricots and olives,
saplings of plants that may or may not grow here,
seeds and coins. Their hands that bear the stain of labor,
lovingly hold their children. They speak words we
don't understand, but there is grace in their speech
and beauty in the treasures they bear for your majesty.

We will open the gates for their visit, so they gather
in the shade of the palace courtyard and await your presence.
We bow to you, sire, lord of the Keral coast, master of our
blessed land of Parasurama who continues to bless us.

Gifting and Receiving

Take this piece of
land, name it, and carry out
your business, build your
temple, care for
your children, may you have
many, and live among Arabs
Christians, Syrian Christians
Hindus and Buddhists on
this Keral land divinely blessed
and be with us as one. Go in peace
my brothers and sisters.

*

If we can call a square piece
of land our own, name it
plan the streets, houses, temple
and businesses

walk in and out of a door
smell the morning breezes
from a window, watch birds
scatter across the sky

you cannot imagine what
these mean to us who have
traveled the seas from the land
of olives, so thank you.

I Was Seven

That's me, standing between Baba and Amma,
barely reaching my mother's hip,
my tight plaits sporting red ribbons
tied into bows. See me running in and out
of the synagogue, my frilly frock fluffing out
in the wind? How excited I am to be in a celebration:
Amma in a silk sari, her hair in a bun, Baba
in a suit like his friends. The doors of the synagogue
are open. People gather on the street. No one
tells me, "Stop running. Sit down. Mind your
brothers." Those annoying boys are at home
with the maid. And I am free to explore. Oh,
there is so much gold and red in this temple,
the tall lamps are lit and multicolored glass dance
their hues on the windows. How strange
the objects in the room—the tall table, the big book,
the writing on the walls. I do not even know
what building we're in until Amma explains,
"It is a synagogue, a Jewish temple." I carry the sound
of my light steps, velvet in my eyes.

Solomon's Awakening

Soft sing-song intonations of the Hebrew Bible
float in through the window in the breezes from the jetty.

Where is the singing coming from?
Familiar strains in a strange tongue.

I am transported to the gardens of Babylon,
lounging with my beloved, tasting her fruit.

Ah, love, sweeter than wine. A door opens in my heart
and I am in the temple under the Star of David.

Centuries of being away from home makes me thirsty.
Quenched, I will call these unfamiliar walls my own.

Definition

When you are given a piece of ground,
you name it first,
then you place one brick, then another,
add an arch,
a terrace,
pave a path,
hang a symbol.
If there is a blue sky,
your structure gains a form
that fits the name.

Esther Hosts her Sisters in Kochi Synagogue

She stands behind a row of chairs, dressed in orange.
Her ancestors' odyssey was blessed in orange.

Sunlight falls within these walls in wide arcs.
Even in shadow, her welcome is gazelle-orange.

In full-sleeved churidhar kameez she smiles like Kochi harbor
At her sisters who've come from deserts bruised orange.

Guests hold plastic cups filled with apple juice and Seven-Up.
I sip my soda mystified how history cruised the globe's orange.

The synagogue fills with Malayalam, Hebrew, and English.
But the Shabbat unites, starched linen or pressed orange.

Outside, police jeeps under dark leaves guard the temple.
No one knows how violent thoughts manifest in orange.

I have come by way of paper lanterns marking my path.
What is this other shadowing me? Night in misted orange.

"Esther," they call her, jasmine studding their auburn curls.
When she speaks, her voice is laughter-glazed orange.

Evening Song

Place the menorah in the center
light the seven stems one by one
the glow grows and spreads around us
our hearts are lit with its core.

The warmth of evening flows out
toward the sea with its merry trove
sunset brings the water's message
filling our house with love.

Place the menorah in the center
light its seven stems one by one
the beloved graces our table
lifting our hearts to the one most High.

For eyes to see this light
For the fresh air we inhale
For birds chirping their delight
For the honey of life, we thank you.

Love

> *Oh, beautiful as the moon,*
> *Like a dove...*
> *Arise, shine,*
> *For the light hath come—*
> *"Yafah Ca Levanna," Wedding Song*

If you measure the current
between two

one standing in a latticed gallery
looking down
at the profile of a man—

he glances up
and she catches his dark eyes
the dimpled chin

but he only sees shadows
above in the women's gallery
not the sculpted
face, her struck heart—

if indeed you were to measure
this current
you would enter heaven.

Torah Scrolls

Filigreed cylinders—
silver leaves and flowers—
with crowns on their heads.

Gold crowns—an offering
by the Raja of Travancore,
for he knew the worth
of guarding the sacred store.

Only blessed fingers can
open the heart like a jar,
and let mundane moments slip
into the ineffable.

*

We know why mystery
is stored, its syllables
rich with darkness,

for to unveil it
would make the everyday
ordinary.

What is life
without expectation of
the ultimate revelation?

From Israel to Kochi

Conference of Israeli scholars,
held in Tekumbagum Synagogue, Eranakulam, March 2009

They have come from Israel
to breathe the same air as their people
once breathed. Along the sands of Kochi
they walk, their eyes mirroring
the slate blue sky filling the water
lined by catamarans, Chinese fishing nets
and poles dividing sunsets and sunrises.

They have come from Israel
to turn over their ancestors' sacred goblets
and vases in their hands, feel
the Torah handled through many services,
taste the Shabbat meal served on banana leaves—
rice, fish kozhombu, pineapple wedges.

They have come from Israel to walk
Jew Town that winds past the aqua walls of shops
selling oriental carpets and trinkets
towards the clock tower, grind grainy sand
of the synagogue compound under
their bare heels as they look up at the roof of sky,
feel the cool blue printed Chinese tiles,
gaze at the gold pulpit with its velvet drape
around the slim gold pillars,
raise their eyes to square prints on the ceiling,
glass chandeliers like fiery trees,
silk drapery against the walls, colored
globes of glass waiting to be lit.

Yes, they have come from Israel to decipher
symbols on abandoned pillars, scratch paint
to a surprise of Hebrew lettering,
discover old synagogue walls and Jewish homes
behind the commercial buzz of Kochi.

Do they know now the comfort of succor
among the tumult of the market, in the lazy
rocking of the boats on dreamy water,
in noon stillness before the arrival of crows?

Cemetery

That's how the dead are arranged
in a large field—mound after mound—

As if symmetry helps us swallow
the unbearable. Meena, David, Joseph,

Noah—they hear the winds from Ararat
and Canaan, the Nile and the Black Sea.

Guarded by an iron gate, menorahs carved
into its bars, the dead keep an eye on the synagogue

welcoming the next visitor carried through
the blue door. When the cemetery gates creak open,

each generation passes into history
in a fraction of time.

A pad on my lap, I sketch the synagogue.
Children gather, watch my strokes come alive.

One boy says, "Draw me," posing, smiling,
a hand on his bony hip, imagining his film hero.

My eyes trace his form, the temple's aqua door
framing him. I hear his mother call, *Mon evada poi?* Son, where are you?

How many mothers look for their children in the billowing waves?
How many young ones search for their parents?

Hagglers in the bazaar grow distant. Even the crows are quiet.

Double Podia

Since Paradise is a mystery
one has to play with bricks and tiles
carve wood, stand slabs of floor
on pillars dipped in gold
always aiming toward the clouds.
We stepped up to look across the ocean
westward
then slowly shifted our gaze
skyward.   We learned to depend

on the lull between rains: Hailing a taxi
or huffing to the bus stop, rushing an errand
for fish or attending *brit milahs*
before the onslaught, plucking ripe fruit,
delaying rot. Naming, lighting the Shabbat lamps,
comforting the one whose child is lost at sea.

The Clock Tower

Solomon looks up at the clock tower
above the synagogue.
Time for a stroll, he thinks,
before the sizzle of afternoon sun.
Hebrew numerals on the clock face
make him believe he is in Jerusalem.
He knows Abdul feels the same when he
glances at the east side of the clock tower
with its Arabic numerals.
The Raja from his palace takes the Malayalam
dials on the clock for granted as he lifts
up his chin before his next *darbar* meeting.
Only the British care about the Roman
numerals as they arrive in the port
to carry out their business. It is not
a spiritual matter, the language of time.

1943-1945

Auschwitz, Dachau, Bergen-Belsen.
The pictures mocked us,
You cannot pretend you are not us,
can you?

Black and white photos framed by newsprint
spread out on the hall table. Not many reports,
but enough for us to know that Jews
were being gassed by the Nazis.

Could it happen to us? Here?

We did not foresee Partition,
tributaries of blood running into our harbor.

We did not make waves. We went about
our business. We remained silent.
We served the country.

Inauguration of the 400th Anniversary of the Cochin Synagogue, 1968

It was a long sojourn. But within this frame, hanging in my parents'
living room, time is frozen in black and white; the garland's ivory
glistens in my father's hands as he lifts it towards Indira Gandhi.
She holds out her hands to receive it, smiling at him.

Amma stands between them, her round face composed, filled
with the heaviness of celebrity: Everything needed to be in place,
the smile, the distance between her sari and the Prime Minister's,
her hair safely secured in a bun, chief elder Mr. Koder bearing
the weight of history in his girth, standing beside my father.

The sky is just right. No rain. I am not in this photo as I am running
in and out of the synagogue and in the courtyard behind my parents.
But I know a scarlet ribbon stretches taut, ready to be snipped
by royal scissors marking 400 years of passage. Much longer,
say the people, much earlier. It has been a long sojourn.

Between Two Shores

They told stories of our people in exile. How it happened. Over and over. The elders were always talking about it. I was laughing and playing with my friends, sang on Shabbat evenings, and helped Ammai with the Pesach meals. To me the stories were simply stories. They did not affect me. They were not real to my life. I was just a happy child, then a happy woman. I wanted to marry, have kids, go to synagogue, and make a good life. But one day I was reading the newspaper and saw pictures of children like skeletons in a camp. Bergen-Belsen in Germany. These could be my children, I thought. These could be me. These are me. I felt tears and rage and passion rise in my belly. A wild cry rose in my throat and I let it out into the monsoon air. I could no longer see my life in one straight line.

*

How can you predict if your neighbor will love you or kill you? How can you predict if you can or cannot stop your desire to extend your home into your neighbor's yard? Your heart says one thing, the holy text another. Your ears are open, but you can't hear. You button up your heart and act. The guide has vanished into the dust hills. You have never tasted sand. You can only feel its acrid grind in your mouth. There is no looking back. Your feet only know to step forward. You spawn kids. You grow gardens. And love, jealousy, anger, and the rest of the deadly sins. Your guilt is a palimpsest layered with want and striving and more want. You can now even kill. That which had built you and which you had nurtured is in the shadows. A miasma. You kiss the ground. You could not have predicted this morphing. Calls to prayer break through walls. You cannot predict how long you will remain intact.

Self-Portrait of a Newcomer

He was as candid as a tree climber
shooting coconuts from the sky:
Here's a piece of land, do what you will,
worship, flourish….
We heeded Raja's words like Torah scrolls.

I heard this story in every wind gust.

Paintings in the temple's foyer
etched our history in our minds:
Never forget: Raja, newcomer, welcome,
gifts, coins, business, peace.

We forgot the desert. Monsoon winds
blew our doors off their hinges.

I replaced a window, then a door, dragged
a fallen trunk off the road, rode my bicycle
to the market, the jetty, the palace, rang
my bell as I swerved around bullock carts
and slow pedestrians. Every Shabbat
I lit the candles and cleaned my nails.

Legend of Mona Lisa

I'm going to keep knocking until you let me in ... d'you hear I'm going to keep on knocking like that woodpecker tut tut tut tut tut till I poke holes into the blasted door that you keep closed to us slaves ... we'll get in that door and speak directly to the One Most High just you wait and watch you *vellakara* stepping over us 'cuz of our darkness ... tho' you know Jehovah sees none o' that ... you'll see you'll hear me Mona Lisa stepping in like it's my own home ... just you watch this Malabari ... I'm going to keep on knocking... my Shekinah my witness making fish leap out of the jetty and the ferries jive in the wind ... I'm just going to keep on keep on...

We produced Salem, our Jewish Gandhi...are your consciences rubbed raw? You can keep your name, Paradesi, but we've been here since the destruction of the Second Temple...what's more, we witnessed the Portuguese setting our synagogue aflame...all this before you moved in and declared you're superior because you're white ... so listen to our Gandhi and throw your attitude into the latrine ... or I Mona Lisa will not tire of rousing up our people.

Naming

      Hmmm. What do I name her if she's a girl?
Golda, after the great Israeli amma? Or Goldy,
more westernized, right, no? Or Indira,
Nehru's daughter? My wife says if it's a boy,
he will be Moses. People should know your identity.
Moses is migaccha admirable, burning bush and all that.

      I want a name with currency, modern.
Daughter with heft. Her words will move worlds.
I want my mol to be a presence
no one will forget. So Golda it will be.

      I see her climb the bamboo ladder to the *mikvah*.
We will sing "Oh Beautiful as the Moon"
when she weds, with wine and seven blessings.
I can already hear her promise
to grow our garden.

Jackfruit Dream

Just like you scale a fish, use your sharpest knife
to slice away the prickly epidermis, then gut it
like you would disembowel a goat, stir molasses
on a hot stove and mix the sacs of fruit
into the sticky syrup, along with cardamom
and cashew; the steam rising out of the mixture
will carry you beyond the deserts of Arabia, I swear,
even if I am not supposed to, oh, god god god,

just you do it the way I tell you, so we have
a successful seder; we want our friends
to recite the sacred words of escape from Egypt
and enjoy a good meal, taste your *chakaravarati*,
its sweet relief after the perilous journey.

Alphabet

That's how the letters looked—
like tree branches, some gnarled,
some bent, some straight.
Until she sounded them into words
they inhabited the abstract world where
mysteries dwelled.

Her eyes moved from right to left,
as she collected the twiggy letters
and sounded them out Shalom
Challah, concretizing them so I could
taste them in my mouth, feel their breath
from my gut, marry the sound.

Malayalam was a land of curlicues—
snails, snakes, jellyfish, letters with no backbone.
They stayed somnambulant. When energized from slumber
they produced melody. Kashnam, manslayi, samayam
curled my tongue around themes of m's and y's.
Between branches and snails, I grew up with Hebrew
in the synagogue and Malayalam at home.

Dear Papa

I'm enjoying the swift pace of Bombay,
its British-built trains slithering in different directions
from Victoria Terminus. I can set my watch by their
arrivals and departures. But I miss the slow pace of home

carrying us through morning blessings of pomfret
in the market, Alia's endless tirades, fishermen dragging
home their trove, evening prayers in the synagogue, ammai's
fish kozhambu, rice and appam.

Here I mostly eat pao bhaji or poori sabji in an Iranian restaurant
opposite my bank. I found a synagogue here. Although the service
is in Marathi, it is the only place that feels like home. Tell Ammai
I will visit during the High Holidays. Affly, Noah.

Dear Noah

I am relieved you're working in a bank
instead of fighting for the British in the East Indies
or in Europe. Even though you're far away, you
are safe and busy. In Kochi there are no jobs,
but this will change since the country is industrializing.

Foreign banking will emerge as a new territory, a reverse
colonialism wouldn't you say, son? But, let's drop politics.
I am glad you found a synagogue. You will make new friends
and learn more about the Bene Israel. We have a couple of
cousins who married into those families. Send me photos
of the sights. Your affectionate, Papa.

P.S. Next door Abdullah has left for Saudi.
Not on pilgrimage to Mecca, but for work.
Amina says his prospects look good there;
they can now build extra room for their newborn.
I miss chatting with him in the evenings,
arguing about politics. Since he is away,
only Ammai can visit the family.

She says Amina hides her emotions well.
Good food and heavy hearts don't make
a full belly is what I say.

Desert Experiment
Next year in Jerusalem

As the land that was promised took more than it was offered,
my grandchildren flew to the Negev,
the desert wind drying the monsoon from their skin.

They write, "Thatha, you should visit. You will meet many of
our faith from different countries. The variety of us is
a permanent rainbow.

We are growing a garden of blooms in the desert.
Roses, bougainvillea, you won't believe it."

I am skittish about bombs. Why would I leave
my peaceful harbor for the threat of gunfire?

I want to wake up to crows calling
and sleep to crickets cleaning their throats.

This is nirvana. That one is a wish
trying out its fledgling wings.

History

The past, the way back past, is frozen.
Most of us hacked it a few times,
but it did not give.

A few flat, frosted dents blossomed
on its opaque surface.

We gave up soon, for the daily called us urgently
to attend to each passing minute.

First survival, then desire, finally ambition.

We became like the rest.
Now that we are the rest, there is no "rest."

Those who left for Israel look back.
Soon they will stop looking
back.

Just like in the afterlife, no one
says, "Oh, I want to go back,"

knowing full well the passage will be the same:
shuffling one's way to the afterlife.

Our Days Are Like Passing Shadows

—Psalm 144:4 Inscription on the
Paradesi Synagogue Clock Tower

She stands at the counter, thin sunlight falling across her face,
Handing out tokens for the rupees we slip into her hand.

Pale among the chalk walls of the courtyard, she counts the money,
Puts it in a steel box, and waits for the next tourist to walk in.

"No camera. Leave it here," she orders, protecting her one sacred space.
The ultimate cannot be captured on celluloid.

I don't photograph her either. I am afraid of invading her world.
The red gold draperies and the colored chandeliers beckon me

To imagine the songs sounding brokenly to the one most High
Voices invoking the Promised Land, shaping it ceremoniously

For centuries, some say, since the time of Solomon. I'm a passing
Shadow among the pews, my pen barely grazing the page, my thoughts
Barely registering the years of worship, argument, and love.

The counter stands empty when I leave. I pick up my camera,
Find no trace of her figure, her cotton dress, outside the door.

Field Trip

Girls in black burqas stroll about the synagogue,
their teacher takes attendance: Fatima, Jamila,
Ajan. Some scribble in their notebooks,
balancing them in the crook of their elbows.

One draws on a piece of paper
the gold Hebrew inscription by the red drapery,
while her friend beckons, *Ivada va.*

Some giggle, or whisper, their headscarves
framing their secrets. Silence, the sign
at the door exhorts. Time to go.

They wander around the compound,
wear their sandals left by the door,
don't stop to gaze at the hall of paintings
of Rajas and their Jewish subjects.

Running past vendors selling trinkets,
shopkeepers calling, *Want to look at carpets?*
They reach the jetty to catch the ferry home.

The teacher strides ahead, the trip crossed off
his list like a black railing. Behind them
the star of David where the road drops.

Triptych
> *(paintings in the Cochin Synagogue)*

Arrival

In Cranganore, cuckoos anchor the day,
bright for ivory and spices. Tusks lean whale-heavy
against hutment walls luring sailors from Palestine
via Yemen. Odor of fish hangs heavy.
> In a white dress, her shoulders caressed
> by sea wind, she leans against a stack of logs,
> watching immigrants in ochre robes
> navigate past basking cows and dogs to
> carry out business, gesturing with their hands.

Beyond coconut trees and elephants, in the port
wives wait with their babies for their husbands.

Another Exile

Oh, the sea turns a deep blue,
the blue of urgency. We don't despair.
> The sea has rescued us from the Portuguese
> torching our homes in Cranganore,
> beaching us here on Cochin sands.

Gifts pour in. We draw stars on wet mud,
follow footprints of the Raja's men
from the palace to our homes. Later,
Ma Navu al heharim, how beautiful
upon the mountains rocks us to sleep.

Domestic

Sing the parrot song,
she begs her mother on Purim.
> They dance around the room,
> stepping to *palote pazham tharuven painkiliye.*

At night, the little girl dreams of her dear bird
pecking at a dessert of milk and banana.
> The moon's rim lights the clouds.

We are Not a Museum

The whole world seems to have landed on our doorstep.
How did this happen? Yesterday a woman was peeping
into my bedroom. Now I close my doors and windows
to keep out nosy tourists creeping around Mattancherry.

A journalist called asking me about my life in Kochi.
I said it is like any other woman's. I have a huge load
of laundry to wash, dishes to scrub, chickens
to pluck. I'll rest only in the grave. So goodbye.

I don't care if they think we are strange or important.
It is absurd. We're like any other Indian in this town
struggling to make life better for our children. I want
the lot of them out of this town and out of our lives.

Movement

We're back,
on ancient soil.

We answered the call,
hearing it

through conflagration &
the muezzin's tune.

From Shabbat to Shabbat
we strain to heed words
spoken before time.

In this brown land
we dance to film songs,

plant gladioli and roses
of Malabar,

keeping our ears trained
to a peace we knew.

Immigrating to Israel

Beyond the Holy Wall that soaks up tears
is the familiar tan frown of day

accompanying our brave
trips to the mall. Hear

the kaching-kaching of coins
building routine.

*

Our illusion was rent moments
after our feet touched the ground.

Our instincts kicked into gear.
We had entered other borders,

counted priceless privileges,
gathered blooms among thorns,

so this journey is our promise
fulfilled. But, rest is still at bay.

*

Who will remember the land
we left after our oldest dies?

We learned to look ahead.
In dreams we smell fish squirming

in baskets beside iron scales
and weights, odor of rain,

hear crows caterwauling at twilight,
shutters rattling close.

Against Erasure

L'shanah ha-ba'ah b'Cochin
('Next year in Cochin'), Nathan Katz

Years ago I had left Cochin, and I returned
when its name changed to Kochi. Her Jewish
people are a fine lacework as waves recede.
If you find a jawbone in the new foundation,
please return it to the rightful owner for re-burial.

Ich habe uberall gesucht, yells a young woman,
cycling hard to keep up with her partner. Maybe
they are looking for a restaurant, but the German grates
eerily against the refrain, *Enni enni thirtha dinam* still sung
celebrating British departure from Palestine in 1948.

Someone says, *We are lucky to have a minyan.*
On my way to the service, a shopkeeper begs,
You will look beautiful in this scarf, aunty.
I bark, *do I look like your aunty?*
I do the touristy thing—I buy a thumb-length
of lace for $200 because I believe
it is the last of its kind made by two octogenarian
Italian weavers. I imagine a bride wearing their
artwork, serenaded by percussion and pipes.

My bones are as creaky as those ferry boats,
an elderly man complains, tired of repeating his story.
I ask him why the Chinese tiles in the Paradesi synagogue
show ships with ballooning sails, the pandemonium
of commerce, willow and monasteries lining exotic
shores. *Those are holy, too,* he says.
I recall *sarvam khalvidam Brahma,*
everywhere is Brahman. We are racing against
time, intone anthropologists, archiving every
letter and coin, for memory is unreliable.

My eyes hungrily scan fragments of the past
mixed with the present. I know, when the ferry drops
me off on the opposite shore, words will evade my pen.

9 781646 628278